Wolfgang Amadeus Mozart

WHO WAS...

Wolfgang Amadeus Mozart

The boy who made music

GILL HORNBY

Illustrations by Alex Fox

✳ SHORT BOOKS

First published in 2006 by
Short Books
15 Highbury Terrace
London N5 1UP

10 9 8 7 6 5 4 3 2 1

A CIP catalogue record for this book
is available from the British Library.

Illustration copyright © Alex Fox 2006
Quiz by Sebastian Blake
ISBN 1-904977-64-2

Printed in Great Britain by
Bookmarque Ltd, Croydon, Surrey

To Holly, Charlie, Matilda and Sam of course.
And also to Poppy Gunnerud and Esther Watson.
With love.

*O*n a crisp, clear, winter's morning, with no warning at all, a terrible earthquake ripped a giant hole through the city of Lisbon. As the people ran, screaming for their lives, a giant tsunami rose up over the coast and swept right over them. One hundred thousand people were killed. Many of them, and much of their city, had vanished without trace: flushed down into the bowels of the earth. Lisbon was completely destroyed.

As the new year of 1756 dawned, all of Europe was in a state of shock. There was a sense of change — a whiff of danger — in the air. The Church had been ruling with its iron rod for centuries. Now people started to ask questions. If God ruled the world, why did He do that to Lisbon?

Suppose He was just watching everything, rather than actually running it? Perhaps the scientists could explain the earthquake better than the priests? Should people start looking after themselves and each other, and stop leaving everything up to God? It was the beginning of what we now call The Age of Enlightenment — a time which changed everything, from politics to music.

In the pretty little Austrian city of Salzburg, a violin teacher called Leopold Mozart was anxious. He had a lot to feel anxious about. He was poor, and he was ambitious. He knew that the world around him was changing, and he was keen to understand it. "We live in a century during which we will hear many new things," he said. Whatever this new age was about, he — Leopold Mozart — planned to make his name in it.

But more worrying than that, his wife was expecting a baby at any moment. She had already given birth to six children. Only one of them had survived. What if the earth beneath Salzburg were to quake? Their tiny apartment was on the third floor. They would all be lost! It was a long, cold, tense winter. At last, at eight o'clock in the evening of the 27th of January Anna Maria Mozart gave birth to a small, but healthy boy. They christened him Johannes Chrysostomus

Wolfgangus Theophilus. But he was to be known, in his lifetime and forever more, as Wolfgang Amadeus Mozart — the composer who took music into the Enlightenment.

CHAPTER ONE

The sound of music rang around the Mozart family all day long. In the mornings, the sweet notes of Leopold's violin would waft through their high apartment at Number 9 Getreidegasse – out of the study, around the small living room, and the one, compact bedroom. It would drift through the wide, open windows and down onto the shoppers in the bustling street below. In the evenings, musical friends would come round and join in – Leopold's colleagues from the court orchestra, the violinist Herr Schatchner. They would settle down in the salon, play their duets and trios and laugh into the night. The people of Salzburg, out for a stroll around the old city walls, or down to the river for a view of the mountains, would hear snatches as they passed – of a brand new piece by Leopold himself, or a more familiar bit of Bach.

The infant Wolfgang did not seem, at first, to take much notice. It was true that, even as a baby, he hated the trumpet – the very sound of one made him scream the roof down. In fact he couldn't take any very loud noise – he would always cover his ears. And a wrong note, or a badly-tuned instrument did seem to make him strangely cross. But his first love, his real passion, was numbers. The air may have been full of the sound of music, but the floor – and the walls, and the furniture and everything Wolfgang could get his hands on – was covered with numbers.

Wolfgang always had a piece of chalk in his hands and, when his dear, slightly muddling mama remembered to give it to him, a piece of slate. And with these, he would make patterns of numbers, shapes, sums and sequences all day long. Perhaps they had a brilliant mathematician on their hands, thought Leopold and Anna Maria, fondly.

Young Wolfgang was certainly a handful. He never

stopped talking, asking questions, from the minute his eyes flew open. What was that for? How does this work? Why did that happen? And do you love me? Do you love me? Are you sure you really love me? Anna Maria found him quite exhausting. But, fortunately for her, Wolfgang's big sister, Nannerl, did love him – to bits – and they could play together happily for hours on end.

Leopold Mozart was one of the top music teachers in Salzburg. He had written a book on how to play the violin – *An Essay on Fundamental Violin Method* – which was very highly thought of. Pupils flocked to the Mozart apartment all the time. And when Nannerl was seven, Leopold decided it was time to teach her some music, too. He sat her down at the clavier in the salon and, almost as soon as the first lesson began, he was gripped with a sense of excitement. This girl was good! She was extremely good! And, after a few more lessons, he began to believe that little Nannerl might even be quite brilliant!

Leopold was a highly ambitious and very frustrated man. He had arrived in Salzburg 20 years before with absolutely nothing. He had taught himself to play the violin, and risen to the position of fourth violinist in the court orchestra, as well as becoming court composer. But these were not giddy heights. Every ruler of every state had his own musicians. Leopold worked for the Archbishop of Salzburg, but they had never got on well. He worked hard, was paid little, respected even less and treated no better than a servant. Could it be that Nannerl's talent could somehow offer him a way out of there?

He immediately set to work with Nannerl. If his daughter was as good as he thought she was, he was not going to waste the opportunity. He started a book, just for her, mostly of minuets, each one more difficult to play than the last. She was to practise daily, and have lessons every afternoon. He would have to let some of his other pupils go, to devote more time to her. He talked over his plans with Anna Maria. There was no time to lose. If that girl was going to fulfil her potential, they had better get cracking.

Nannerl did make rapid progress and her father's hopes began to soar. He called Herr Schatchner in to listen to her. He composed pieces that would suit her fingers and stretch her ability. He plotted her progress every day. Perhaps he was even recording it for posterity? Who knows? But we do know that Leopold was so obsessed with what Nannerl was doing that he didn't, at first, notice what his little boy was getting up to. He did not even see that when Nannerl got up from the clavier, her brother took her place. And that, only three years old and very small for his age, little Wolfgang would sit there alone picking out thirds on the keyboard – Nannerl noticed that he particularly liked the sound of a third – and striking out a simple tune.

The moment that he discovered the wonders of that clavier in the corner of the salon, Wolfgang dropped his obsession with numbers. And he stopped asking all those difficult questions. He now just had the one: Why can't I learn the clavier, too? Please, please, please!

Leopold at first refused. After all, the boy was still so tiny and his hands no bigger than a doll's. But Nannerl was on her brother's side. She had noticed quite how keenly he was listening in while she was having her lesson. She had also noticed that, when he

14

was just fiddling around at the clavier on his own, he was picking out what sounded almost like a tune. And an original, rather pretty tune at that...

"Please Papa," she begged. "Please let him learn." Smiling fondly, Leopold gave in. He held out the clavier seat, tiny Wolfgang jumped up and their first lesson began.

Chapter Two

One Thursday evening, Herr Schatchner walked home with Leopold after church. The two men blustered into the study, in need of a quiet drink, to find little Wolferl (as his family affectionately called him) at his father's desk, in the most terrible mess. There were bits of screwed-up paper all over the place and ink, gallons of the stuff, everywhere: Wolfgang's face, his hands, his clothes, the desk were covered. A furious Leopold demanded to know what Wolfgang thought he was doing.

The little boy, without even looking up, calmly replied that he was composing a concerto for the clavier, but he couldn't show it yet, because it wasn't ready. Leopold picked up the pages that were lying there – of scrawled notes and smudges and blots of ink – and showed it to his friend. Both men began to laugh. But then Leopold looked more closely. And he saw that, beneath the childish mess, there was a serious piece of music written down here. The laughter died, and tears came to his eyes: "Look, Herr Schatchner, how properly and correctly it has been written! Only it can't be used. It is so very difficult that no one could play it!" Wolfgang, still looking down at his page and scribbling away, gave an impatient sigh: "That is why it is a concerto, papa. You must practise it until you get it right."

From the minute that he started his lessons on the clavier, Wolfgang's progress had been astonishing. By his fourth birthday, he could play eight of the minuets in Nannerl's book, plus another allegro. Nannerl noted that, after about half an hour's work, he could play a piece "faultlessly, with utmost neatness and exact time." The children still liked to play together. They loved to play marbles in the courtyard down below, or a board game in the snug of their living room. They had a pet canary – which sang on a G sharp, Wolfgang could not help noticing. When they needed to clear up their toys at the end of the day, they would form a marching band, and pipe and drum them from one room to another.

But for Wolferl, playing the clavier was just as much as fun. Once he had mastered a piece, he then liked to improvise on it: pick up the composer's theme and "take it for a walk" until he had turned it into a different piece of music altogether. And all the time, he would laugh with glee, as if he was having the best time in the world.

He adored the evenings when Leopold invited his musical friends round. Even if Wolferl and Nannerl had been put to bed first, he loved to lie in the dark and listen to the sounds from the salon. "That fiddle is an eighth too low," he would whisper to his sister. Or "That should have been a D Major." But when the trumpets joined in, he would hide under the covers.

One such evening, when Leopold, Herr Schatchner and a colleague were going to try out some new string trios, they were surprised to see the four-year-old Wolfgang pottering into the salon. A friend had just presented him with a tiny violin, to fit his tiny shoulder and, although he had not actually tried the instrument yet, Wolferl had decided that tonight he too would join in with the playing. "Absolutely not," said his father, firmly. "These are some of the finest musicians in the city, and you have not even had a lesson yet! To bed with you. Now!" But, as so often happened, Wolferl's tears and storming fury were such that Leopold had either to give up the idea of playing at all, or let the little boy join in. "Alright, alright! If you must… Come and play second fiddle behind Herr Schatchner, but quietly mind! We don't want you ruining the whole thing…"

The strange ensemble – three big men and one,

minute little chap – began. And with astonishment, Herr Schatchner quickly began to realise that he was not needed at all. Wolfgang was playing, note perfectly, a piece he had never seen before on an instrument he had never played. Schatchner put down his own fiddle, and for the rest of the performance just watched and listened. This boy of Leopold's might be badly behaved but – by god! – he was a marvel.

Only when the six trios were finished did Wolfgang look up from the music. He had been so lost in what he was playing that he had not noticed he was playing second fiddle alone. Gosh, that had been fun! "Can we do it all again?" he cried. "Can I play First Violin this time?" The men – bewildered and intrigued by the boy before them – agreed. Again, Wolfgang gave a brilliant performance and was met with a shower of praise. "But now it's bed-time," said Leopold firmly and, for once, Wolfgang did as he was told.

Every night, from when he was a toddler until he was 12, Wolfgang went through the same routine with his Papa. Leopold would plonk Wolferl on a chair; Wolferl would sing a sweet song – *"Oragna fiagat fa"*; Papa would sing it back; and then Wolfgang would kiss his father on the nose. It was a ritual that for some odd reason was crucial to Wolfgang, and if Leopold tried to break it, there was trouble.

There was often trouble in the Mozart household, and it always came from Wolfgang. He was small and pale and sickly, and very highly strung. He made beautiful music, but he could also throw deafening tantrums and Leopold was never quite sure how to handle him. Sometimes, when Wolfgang asked, "Do you really love me?" for the tenth time that day, Leopold would be tempted into saying "No!" Whereupon the child would cry fit to burst and it would take an age to calm him down.

Leopold also gave short shrift to this nonsense of Wolferl hating the trumpet. For heaven's sake, the boy wasn't going to make it as a musician if he couldn't listen to a horn section! He plotted that Herr Schatchner should one day come up behind Wolferl and blow his trumpet into the boy's ear. That would sort him out. It was not a success. Wolfgang immediately turned pale and sank to the floor.

Another second, Schatchner feared, and he would have a convulsion.

That night of the violin performance, after the boy had gone to bed, the adults sat up and talked about him. Leopold showed them his notebook. It was the one that he had started to keep for Nannerl, but which was now mostly about Wolfgang. Beneath a complicated scherzo by Wagenseil, Leopold had written "This piece was learned by Wolfgang three days before his fifth birthday, between 9.00 and 9.30 in the evening." By a minuet and trio, "This piece was learned by Wolfgang within half an hour a day before his fifth birthday." On the 4th of February he had learned a march; on the 6th, another scherzo. And then, between February and March he had composed two pieces which Leopold had written down.

Leopold Mozart and his musician friends were all men of the Enlightenment. They liked to think of themselves as open-minded and cultured. They believed in God, but they also believed in common sense. They had no time for the superstitions and nonsense that the Church wanted to believe in. They were clever and rational and philosophical. But now Leopold was putting aside all that. His boy, he announced to his friends that night, was nothing short of a miracle. A musical miracle. God did, after all, make miracles and He had decided to make one in Salzburg. And it was obviously Leopold's duty to God to go out and convince the world that miracles did exist, and that little Mozart was one of them.

And, while he spoke of God and miracles, he was, at the same time, somewhere in the back of his mind, calculating how miraculously rich and famous this could make them all…

Pretty quickly, Wolfgang's genius took over Leopold's life. Herr Mozart was still employed as a musician at court but, as everyone at court was beginning to notice, he really wasn't very interested in his job any more. He gave up all his other pupils. Instead, he spent his every available minute with Nannerl and Wolfgang. He was their only teacher, not just in music but in every subject. He worked with them on the clavier, at the violin, and on reading, writing and numbers. But he noticed, with Wolfgang, that while he needed to teach him everything else – especially manners! – he did not really need to teach him music. It all seemed to be in that little head already. By his sixth year, Wolfgang was composing more and more. As fast as the music poured out of the little boy, his father wrote it all down in the back of his notebook. It is thanks to that notebook that we have some very famous pieces, like the *Minuet in C* and *Minuet in G*, which are still played today.

So his brilliant children were keeping him pretty busy. And when Leopold wasn't teaching and transcribing, he was plotting: plotting and scheming how best to launch his little treasures onto an amazed, grateful – and hopefully generous – public.

Leopold was dazzled by Wolfgang's progress, but he was also canny. He realised that part of the wonder of his small son came from quite how small he was. This tiny figure, whose hands could not yet stretch five notes, reaching over the clavier and giving a virtuoso performance was indeed an amazing thing to behold. Part of the "miracle" was to hear that music come out from such a form. Once he started to grow, he would look a bit less wonderful. It was crucial to get him to perform to as many people as possible while he was still cute. The Mozarts must go on tour.

Chapter Three

L eopold was keen to get on the road as soon as possible. So confident was he of success, he borrowed money from his landlord to rent a rather smart coach. He hired Herr Estlinger as a valet and bag carrier. And on the 18th of September, 1762 the chattering, excited family climbed aboard and set out to make its fortune.

At their first stop, they were met with almost total indifference. The Prince-Bishop of the city of Passau was very cool about the Mozarts' arrival on his patch. They had to send word several times, over several days, to beg permission to play before him. After a long wait, he eventually consented to hear Wolfgang,

26

but not Nannerl. And at the end of the performance that was supposed to have astonished him, he tipped them with one measly ducat.

"Who needs Passau?" was Leopold's response to that, and on they went. They travelled down the Danube, to the much more grateful city of Linz and here things started to pick up. It was at the Trinity Inn, in Linz, that the first ever recorded public concert by Nannerl and Wolfgang Mozart took place. The crowd loved them, and in that crowd were an important Count and Countess. They reported the

wonders that they had seen to the Archduke Joseph. Word of the Mozarts was already beginning to spread to high places.

Little Wolfgang was proving to be an easy traveller. He and Nannerl were having such fun on the journey: they had invented a wonderful game, creating their own kingdom. He rarely looked out of the coach windows – he wasn't interested in views or places. But he did love meeting all these new people. He was never shy with anyone and loved it when they liked him. When the Mozarts arrived in Vienna by the post boat, Wolfgang played the fiddle at the customs barrier. The officers were charmed and the family's luggage was immediately waved through.

Vienna was the capital of all Austria. It was where the Emperor Francis I lived with his Empress Maria Theresa and their 16 charming children. It was not only a beautiful city, it was also the centre of fashion and of culture. Leopold knew that if his children could make it there, they'd make it anywhere. They arrived on the 6th of October.

Right from the start, the visit was a triumph. On the 9th of October, Wolfgang gave his debut performance – on the clavier at the house of an aristocrat. The crowd went wild. Suddenly every door in the city – however high, however gilded – was opened. The children played to nearly all the counts, chancellors and bishops in the place. Leopold was thrilled to bits.

"Everywhere", he wrote home to his landlord "the ladies are in love with my boy. We are common talk in all places." Their schedule was hectic: one day the French ambassador, the next Count Harrach. People took to booking them for parties four or five days in advance. The grandees would send their beautiful carriages to collect them. "On one occasion", reported Leopold, "we were at a place from half past two to nearly four o'clock; then Count Hardegg sent his carriage for us, which took us full gallop to the house of a lady, where we stayed till half past five; afterwards we were with Count Kauntz till near nine." And little six-year-old Wolfgang had to perform at every stop.

It wasn't long before the Mozarts found themselves walking through the highest, most gilded door of all, when the Empress Maria Theresa invited them to play before her at the summer palace. Leopold was lost for words, but his son was quite undaunted. In the imposing imperial hall, in front of the assembled courtiers in their smartest clothes and their powdered wigs, Wolfgang leapt into the lap of the Empress and smacked a hearty kiss upon her cheek. Leopold's heart leapt into his mouth; all the courtiers fell silent: had the boy already gone too far? But no. Maria Theresa was delighted by this new discovery. When he wasn't playing something marvellous, he was saying something extraordinary. What a diverting little fellow he was! The family was invited back to the palace again and again.

Leopold Mozart was in heaven. There he stood, in the throne room, watching his own children perform to the cream of Vienna. There he smiled, while the whole court applauded their flawless performance. There he made small talk, with the Emperor himself — two fathers chatting together. "This is it!" he thought to himself. "This is how it should be!"

And while his parents were star-struck by their new, grand surroundings, Wolfgang felt instantly at home. All the Emperor's children were extremely friendly to him, and he treated them as equals. One day, two of the little princesses were leading him up to the Empress and he slipped on the highly-polished floor. One of the princesses showed no concern at all, the other picked him up and made a fuss of him.

"You are very kind," he announced to her in front of her mother, "I will marry you." She and her mother laughed together, but they would have done well to accept. That princess was to grow up to be Queen Marie Antoinette of France, and have her head chopped off.

Emperor Francis I was a man in need of constant entertainment. He was delighted with Wolfgang; he called him his "little magician". But, as one always does with a magician, he longed to catch him out. On one occasion, after a splendid performance of a concerto, he covered the keyboard with a cloth. "Let us see how you play now!" he challenged Wolfgang. Wolfgang just laughed and played, as ever, to perfection. Then the Emperor covered Wolfgang's eyes with a blindfold, commanded him to play with one finger, gave him an impossible piece to sight-read, demanded an improvisation. Little Mozart found himself having to name the note of a bell or a clock or a watch. He was treated as part musician, part freak show. But he didn't mind. He performed every party trick and passed every test that was put to him. As long as he was the centre of attention, he was happy. He loved making music, and he really, really loved bowing – again and again – to an enraptured crowd giving him thunderous applause.

He was never in awe of the royal family. One of the princes dared to play the violin to the Mozarts; at the end, all that the unimpressed Wolfgang could say, in a bored voice, was: "That was out of tune." One afternoon, he was to play the clavier in a difficult concerto by Wagenseil. The Emperor sat himself next to Wolfgang to turn the pages for him – a great honour for which the little boy was not grateful. "Where is Wagenseil?" he demanded. "Fetch him to turn the pages for me. He will understand it!" The Emperor was duly dismissed.

But, however spoiled and brattish Wolfgang's behaviour became, it did not seem to matter. He was so small, so sweet, so funny, so brilliant – he was the darling of all Vienna. The Empress presented

Wolfgang with a gold and lilac silk suit that had been made for the Archduke Maximilian; Nannerl was given an ornate gala dress worn by an archduchess. They had been given one hundred ducats to pay for their stay. The French ambassador was talking about an invitation to Versailles. Leopold kept pinching himself. It seemed as though nothing could go wrong...

And then it did. It went wrong, in fact, on two fronts. First of all, back in Salzburg, people at court were beginning to mutter. Where was that Leopold Mozart? Was he still touting those poor children about? Had he forgotten he was supposed to have a proper job? Leopold knew that he was storing up trouble for himself at home, but things were going too well here to waste. He wanted to squeeze everything he could out of Vienna. He would work Wolfgang till he dropped.

And then Wolfgang dropped. After a hectic afternoon with the Empress, he started a high temperature. He got a cold and a rash. A bright scarlet rash. Just as he had hit the peak of his success, he was struck down with scarlet fever. Leopold sent word to all of the boy's fans that he was ill. He expected presents, he hoped for money. He got the cold shoulder. Disease was the terror of the age. The Empress had 16 children. She did not want fever at court. Wolfgang spent a few weeks in bed alone, and Leopold spent 50 of their hard-earned ducats on doctor's fees.

As soon as he possibly could, Leopold got Wolfgang out of bed and back in front of his public. They had had such a success, it would be terrible if everyone just forgot them now. On the 5th of November, a pale Wolfgang Mozart was performing again. He was so frail and weak, his little body had to be propped up at the keyboard with cushions. The audience was quite shocked; the Empress was disgusted. They began to look on Leopold in a whole new light: not so much a proud papa, more a pushy parent.

The Mozarts arrived back in Salzburg in early January – quite famous, but not even nearly rich.

CHAPTER FOUR

After the delights of Vienna, Salzburg was harsh reality. The post of Master of the Chapel had become vacant while the Mozarts were away. It was a job Leopold had been hoping for for years, but it had been given to someone else in his absence. He was made Deputy Master of the Chapel instead. It was fair enough after he had been swanning around Europe for weeks on end, but still he was bitter. And his bitterness fuelled his ambition for his children. They were only home for the winter anyway, he told everyone. They would be touring again soon. "We will depart," he promised his family, "with the arrival of the swallows."

The next time the Mozarts left Salzburg, they did so in style. Herr Mozart's plan was that his children would play to almost all the royal families of Europe. They were to be away for over three years. They had to be comfortable, and they had to look the part. He had bought them a beautiful, gleaming, brand new carriage. He employed a new attendant, Sebastian Winter, whose drawing skills were to prove very useful to the children – they got him to make the map of their imaginary kingdom which still kept them amused on long journeys.

The family trotted off in June 1763, with their heads held high, and had got all of six miles down the road when the wheel of their carriage fell off. Leopold tried to keep cheerful. The weather was lovely. And Wolfgang popped down to the village church while he was waiting and amused himself, and everyone else, by playing the church organ with both hands and feet for the first time. He gave the impression, Leopold wrote home, that "he had been practising in this manner for several months." But still, the omen was not good. The new wheel was horribly expensive. The Mozart European Tour had only been going for a morning, and they were already losing money, not making it.

They arrived in Munich six days later, and got off to a cracking start. The Mozarts had already met the Prince when they had been in Vienna. And Leopold now paraded the children around the palace gardens, in front of the palace windows, until the Prince spotted them and asked them to perform. Wolfgang went on to play before dukes, princes and the Elector himself and wowed them all. But Leopold was getting edgy. He didn't just want adoration — a little payment would also be welcome, thank you very much. The longer these rich royals kept them hanging about waiting to be paid, the more they had to spend on hotel bills and food. It was going to be hard to make any sort of profit if it all went on like this.

They headed off for Stuttgart, the seat of a duke known to be a lavish patron of the arts, but by the time they got there, he had moved off to his summer palace. Having gone that far, the Mozarts decided to follow him out there, but they had not understood what a "summer progress" really meant — that the Duke and his hundreds of supporters and servants all moved house for a few months. It was all such a kerfuffle that the Duke had no time for concerts, or musical tricks. Leopold was kicking himself. He had wasted time, and therefore money, on this detour. He was going to have to get to grips with the practicalities of royal life if he was going to manage these children properly.

In Frankfurt, he went in for some advertising, and it worked. Posters were put up calling to "All those who take pleasure in Extraordinary Things! With Incredible Skill a girl of 12 and a boy of 7 will play Concertos and Sonatas." He added that there would only be one chance to see them – "Paris and London are Waiting!" – and that did the trick. The little Mozarts played to five packed halls in Frankfurt and made a tidy profit.

This tour business brought its fair share of irritations and headaches for Leopold. There was the time they went all the way to Koblenz, only for Wolfgang to take to his bed with a cold. When they got to Bonn, the Elector had just left. At Aix-le-Chapelle, the Princess Amelia thought they were wonderful, but gave them only "kisses, not coins". In Brussels, the Prince kept them waiting for days on end whilst he hunted.

But he was also enjoying himself, a lot. They were travelling in comfort and staying in nice hotels. Good money was coming in from the public concerts. The nobility showered the children with lovely gifts. They had swords and lace and snuff-boxes galore. Prince Charles of Brussels had — eventually — paid them extremely well. Leopold was beginning to feel almost comfortable. He started to buy himself some rather fine clothes; he bought a splendid pair of Mannheim boots. Nannerl had a fabulous wide-brimmed hat which set off her new, teenage beauty. The Mozarts were really quite something.

One November morning, the family slumped, shattered, within their coach as it thundered across northern France. They were in a hurry, and travelling by express, but it was exhausting. "I feel like a soldier in the army of Empire being pursued by two divisions of Prussians," Leopold moaned to the others. Suddenly, he was jolted out of his misery by the excited shouts of his children. Even Wolfgang, who never took any notice of his surroundings, was pointing and gawping out of the window. For there, arising out of the blank, bleak plains was Paris. It was an amazing sight to one who knew only German cities, with their ramparts and walls. And it was the jewel in the crown of their tour – where the Mozarts hoped finally to make their name.

The French court at that time was a difficult nut to crack. King Louis XV lived a complicated life – on the one hand he had his stuffy, fat, devout queen, and on the other his powerful, sophisticated mistress Madame de Pompadour. The trick was to somehow keep in with both sides. Leopold managed to get them all in to meet Madame de Pompadour first, only for Wolfgang to treat her with his typical cheek. He was standing up high on a table, waiting to be introduced, when Madame suddenly changed direction and went to speak to someone else first.

"Who does she think she is?" demanded the seven-year-old loudly, "Not wanting to kiss me? I'll have you know that I have been kissed by none other than the Empress herself!" And he stamped his little foot.

Leopold nearly had a heart attack. It had been a long way to come to insult the most powerful woman in France. The room held its breath while the Madame turned back to him... and exhaled with relief when it saw she was smiling. What a cheeky little fellow! She crossed back to kiss him after all. Both the children were invited to her apartments at Versailles as well as her grand house in Paris, where Wolfgang played on a harpsichord "all in gold leaf, and lacquered and painted with the utmost art".

To his father's joy, Wolfgang did manage to crack the court at Versailles as well. The poor Queen was a sad, bored thing. Her passion for God did not leave much room for passion on any other front (except food – she had been known to eat 180 oysters in one sitting). She needed brightening up, and along came little Wolfgang to do just that. He played the palace organ in front of the whole court. His organ playing was the biggest crowd-pleaser now; he had become brilliant at it, and it was quite a comic spectacle watching this still tiny figure – in his white powdered wig, and a dashing silk suit, with a ceremonial sword at his hip – as the master of such an enormous instrument.

In Paris Wolfgang put on two large public

concerts, and suddenly the Mozarts were all in fashion. A family portrait was engraved, poems were written about them, they were mobbed wherever they went. On New Year's Eve, they were called to the court. They expected to stand with the other courtiers, looking on as their majesties stuffed their faces for hours on end. In fact, they were called to

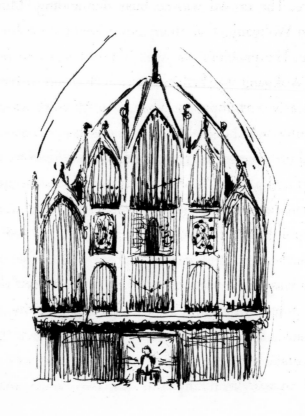

the table. Wolferl spent the evening chatting to the Queen, and eating little offerings from the royal fingertips. It was an undreamed of success.

"The people are all crazy about my children," Leopold wrote home to Salzburg. Actually, he was covering up a shift in the family that had now taken place. Nannerl almost never got to perform any more. The crowd was so busy demanding "More!" from Wolfgang, that there never seemed to be the time. The problem was that Nannerl was excellent, but Wolfgang was brilliant. Nannerl was now twelve – nearly a woman, in those days; Wolferl was just turning eight, and still small for his age. Plus, he did all those fancy tricks, with blindfolds and cloths and bells and clocks. Wolfgang was definitely the draw. When Nannerl did get to perform, it was always Leopold, rather than the audience, who led the applause.

It was on this tour, in Wolfgang's eighth year, while the people of Europe were hailing his playing as a miracle, that another musical miracle began to be revealed. Wolfgang Mozart began to compose. He had always picked around at the keyboard, almost from when he could sit. But it was in this year – first in Paris, then in London – that he properly began to write music.

From Paris, Leopold had written home that Wolfgang's first four sonatas were about to be published. "Imagine the noise these sonatas will make in the world when people read on the title page that they are the work of a child of seven years old... I may tell you that God daily works wonders with this child."

When the family arrived in London, they were met with great warmth by King George II and his Queen, Charlotte. But Wolfgang was more excited to meet the Master of the Queen's music at the time: J C Bach. This Bach, the son of the more famous Johann Sebastian Bach, and a brilliant musician in his own right, was intrigued by this little Austrian wonder. He sat at the clavier, put little Wolfgang between his knees and played a few bars of a melody. Wolfgang continued it for a little, and before long, they had composed a sonata between them, their hands chopping and changing at the keys.

One evening, returning from a concert in the

damp home of an English Lord, Leopold Mozart caught a cold, which became a fever, which soon took him to death's door. The situation was grave, and the children were terrified. Without papa, they were unable to go out and, while he was so ill, they had to keep quiet. In their Chelsea house, that autumn of 1764, while their father lay struggling, the only sounds in the house were the whispers of the children and the scratching of a pen. Wolfgang was overheard giving Nannerl strange instructions: "Remind me to give the horns something to do."

When their father was eventually able to sit up in bed, his children presented him with their own "Get Well" present. Many sheets of paper, scrolled up with a ribbon – it was *Symphony Number One in E flat*, by Wolfgang Mozart. While the house had been quiet, Nannerl had written the whole thing out from Wolfgang's instructions. And Wolfgang had composed all three movements entirely in his head.

When he was a child, Wolfgang had a magpie's approach to composing: that is, he would borrow from, or imitate other musicians he admired at the time. This first symphony shows the influence of J C

Bach and Carl Abel, both men who were working in London then and whom Mozart admired very much. But there are other elements of it which are pure Mozart: it opens with a crashing fanfare, and then goes into a quiet passage. That was a trick he would use for the rest of his life.

At first, London loved the Mozarts, and the Mozarts loved London. They fed the animals in the zoo – Wolfgang was not afraid of the tigers, but he almost fainted at the loudness of their roar – and walked in the parks. They were delighted when the royal carriage passed by and the King and Queen gave them such a friendly wave. Wolfgang wrote a set of sonatas and dedicated them – sensibly – to Queen Charlotte. He was paid a fantastic 50 guineas for that. His *Chelsea Symphony* was put on in concert. "Come and Hear the Prodigies of Nature!" screamed the posters. Everybody flocked.

People were so amazed by the child genius that rumours began that he was not a child at all. An important Professor, Daines Barrington, came to spend some time with Wolfgang, and work out if he was not indeed too good to be true. Wolfgang

CHILD GENIUS
FROM THE
MOUNTAINS
OF
AUSTRIA
OZART

performed all his many tricks on the clavier, which proved he was a genius. And when a cat walked into the room, and he left the keyboard to stroke and pet it, the Honourable Daines Barrington decided that he was indeed a child. He wrote a paper on the subject for the British Museum.

By the spring of 1765, though, the rot had begun to set in. Leopold could see now that there was a pattern to their popularity. People were only interested in Wolfgang for a limited space of time. They, generally, were happy to see him perform just the once. The public's attitude was then, "Been there, done that, that's enough child prodigies for me, thank you very much". It had happened to them whenever they stayed more than a few months anywhere, and it infuriated Leopold every single time. He always turned against the country they were staying in. In one letter to Salzburg he harrumphed: "I am determined not to bring my children up in so dangerous a place as London, where people for the most part have no religion. You would be astonished to see how people are brought up here."

In April, the children were reduced to opening their home to the public on Tuesdays and Fridays from 12 o'clock till 3, when the people could pay to come in and examine their playing, and make them do all the old musical tricks, at close quarters. They were turning into a travelling freak show. It was time to go.

CHAPTER FIVE

Anna Maria Mozart was exhausted, and more than a bit concerned. She was tired of trying to look after her children in rented lodgings and hotel rooms. She was bored of the constant travelling in that exhausting coach. She did not have her husband's ambition or her children's brilliance and, frankly, trying to chat with the crowned heads of Europe was getting a bit wearing. She wanted to go home.

And that was her worry. What was there at home? Would Leopold even have his job when he got back there? News of Wolfgang's triumphal musical progress around Europe had of course reached Salzburg. Perhaps the Archbishop would see the boy as his own property. Was he having all this success, only to become little more than a servant when he returned?

Then there was money. She left all of that side of things up to Leopold – he was so clever about all that. But she couldn't help noticing that this touring business did seem terribly risky. They were spending so much on rent. The children – bless them – had done some wonderful concerts. The money had come pouring in! But they had had to rent the concert halls in the first place and, sometimes, the figures didn't seem quite to add up. They had some incredible presents – snuff-boxes galore! More snuff-boxes, in fact, than they were ever going to have room for when they got home. These grand people, they were so generous with their things. But not so much with money, it seemed. The whole trip had been just marvellous but, as far as she could tell – and what did she know after all? – they were still flat, stony broke.

Anna Maria would have liked to go straight home to Salzburg from London. Leopold had other ideas. They would perform their way back across the continent, cashing in on the fame they had built up on the way through. The Prince of Orange, in Holland, wanted to see them. It would be almost rude not to pop back to the Queen in Paris. They might as well take in the mountains and lakes of Switzerland while they were passing. They finally got back to Salzburg just before Wolfgang's 11th birthday.

***

It is a fact of life that people do not always get much of a kick from the success of others. Leopold Mozart was back in his place in the court orchestra. He and his family were living in their old flat at 9 Getreidegasse. They didn't seem richer, or changed, to the people of Salzburg. But, golly, that Leopold didn't half brag. He went on and on about empresses and queens. It was Wolfgang this, Wolfgang that. Wolfgang had written a splendid symphony for the Prince of Orange. Wolfgang had written an oratorio. Wolfgang had written a set of six sonatas for clavier and violin... All the other court musicians were sick to death of it.

They did not mind the boy himself, though. He

had improved a lot on his travels, though he still giggled too much and got a bit cheeky at times. Since he had been back home, he seemed to be composing more and more. The University commissioned him to write the music for an opera, *Apollo and Hyacinth*. It was performed by the boys at the choir school, accompanied only by Wolfgang himself on the clavier. The audience found it delightful. Pieces for the clavier and violin seemed to be trotting off his pen. The Archbishop himself was intrigued. If he really did have a boy wonder on his patch, then he ought to get him to work, for the glory of himself and his city. On the other hand, he had heard that the boy was a fraud, that it was his father writing it all for him.

At Easter, 1767 the Archbishop required a new mass. It might be the moment to test this young Mozart. So Wolfgang was summoned to the palace, locked up alone in a room with a guard outside his door, and told that he would not be allowed out until he had produced a mass. Anna Maria was beside herself. The boy had never been away from his family before. To be locked up in a room like that – almost a cell! But Wolfgang was perfectly happy. He was being fed and he had work to do. When he was writing, he didn't really notice where he was, anyway. What was all the fuss about?

Five days later, the music was written, Wolfgang was back home and it was liver and dumplings for dinner. The piece was performed to the packed and enormous cathedral in Salzburg on Good Friday, and anyone who doubted Wolfgang Mozart was now silent.

But still, they did not actually long for his success. That September, the Mozarts returned to Vienna, the city which had loved him just a few years before. They were hoping that Wolfgang might get a big commission. Before he could even set to work there, he got small pox. He was dangerously ill. For ten, terrible days he could not even see. When he did recover, his previously cute face was covered in horrible scars.

And when the city finally got back to normal after the outbreak, Leopold found, to his horror, that Wolfgang suddenly had more enemies than friends. Vienna was an important centre for music. The Emperor was all-powerful among musicians. Other composers watched as Joseph II singled out Mozart, and they resented it. Wolfgang was no longer a sweet little boy. He was twelve, and he was soon going to be a threat. No musicians would attend his concerts, and no-one wanted to perform his music.

The Emperor hinted to Leopold that an opera from Wolfgang would be nice. It was just what Leopold wanted, and he took it to be a commission. Wolfgang busied away, and wrote a light opera called *La finta semplice* – or, *The Pretend Idiot*. But the singers and orchestra had no intention of putting it on. They muddled the music and the rehearsals until the whole thing had to be abandoned.

"Envy has broken forth on every side," cried Leopold. "The whole hell of music has bestirred itself to prevent the talent of a child from being known." He was spitting with rage.

The Mozarts returned home.

***

Wolfgang's childhood bedtime routine – of singing to Leopold, and being kissed on the nose – was performed less often now. But he still worshipped the ground that his father walked on: "Right after God comes Papa!" he would chirrup.

The adoration was mutual. While he worked feverishly at the keyboard or writing new pieces, Wolfgang did so under a shower of praise from Leopold. "That was perfect, Wolferl!" "Are you listening to this fugue, mama?", "Wait till the archbishop hears this!" Herr Schachtner disapproved of the way Leopold was bringing him up. The praise seemed to him excessive. Leopold these days was a man obsessed.

In his thirteenth year, Wolfgang was settled happily back into Salzburg life. He was now writing a lot of music – symphonies and dances for his neighbours to enjoy. He had been appointed co-leader of the Salzburg court orchestra – no real money, as yet, but it was recognition. He had a lot of friends in his pretty, Alpine home town and he loved the local dances. They were so much more fun than the balls he had witnessed on his travels to Paris and London. In the big cities, they were still dancing the minuet, gliding slowly alone, keeping each other at arm's length. In Salzburg, couples were spinning and twirling in each other's arms. They had learned to waltz, and were having a wonderful time.

Leopold however had not settled at all. After all the excitements of the royal courts of Europe, he found being back at work pretty humdrum. He kept moaning to Anna Maria: "Why should I stay put in Salzburg, sighing and hoping vainly for a stroke of luck, seeing Wolfgang grow up? Why should my son take his first step in vain, thanks to the Vienna opera, and not even attempt to pursue the path so clearly meant for him?"

And so Leopold's greedy eyes swivelled away from stuffy northern Europe, where they couldn't appreciate a good thing when they saw it. He wanted pastures new, nice sunshine, warm temperaments, artistic people... Italy! He would take Wolfgang to Italy. They'll understand him there. This time, the Archbishop gave the Mozarts his blessing. In December 1769, father and son kissed Anna Maria and Nannerl and set out, just the two of them, together.

CHAPTER SIX

Father and son were perfect travelling companions. Leopold's serious, pernickety, political nature meant that he was brilliant at making travel arrangements, and plotting who they should meet and where Wolfgang should perform. Wolferl was in high spirits: "My heart is filled with alott of joy because I feel so jolly on this trip, because it's so cozy in our carriage and because our coachman is such a fine fellow," he wrote home to his mama. He would often knock out a sonata on the way from one town to another, but he couldn't spell for toffee.

Italy and the Mozarts got on like a house on fire. This was a place where they understood music. When they stopped in a monastery, went to mass in a church, spent a night at the opera or just ate in a piazza, they found beautiful music performed to an impeccable standard.

Leopold was a man of great cultural appreciation. He loved seeing all the artistic treasures which Italy had to offer. In Holy Week, at Easter, the Mozarts were in Rome and went to matins in the Sistine Chapel. The choir there was exceptional, and had one special piece of music of their own. It was called the *Misere* by Allegri. It had never been written down; monks had passed it down to one another, from generation to generation. It was highly complicated, using a double choir, nine parts and a strange rhythm, and it was the Pope's orders that it should never be performed anywhere else.

The Mozarts were honoured to be there and to hear it. That morning, listening to that music whilst looking at Michelangelo's wondrous ceiling, Leopold was transported: it was all so sublime, he thought his heart might break. Wolfgang, however, was reacting differently. Top secret was it, this music? Amazingly complicated? Never to be written down? For the

Sistine Chapel alone? We'll see about that, he thought…

When they emerged into the light, Leopold wiped the tears of emotion from his eyes; Wolfgang giggled wildly. They got back to their lodgings, Wolfgang slammed his door and picked up his pen. That evening, they attended a party together. Leopold was just making small talk with a cardinal when Wolfgang produced some sheet music from his waistcoat with a flourish. There it was, properly annotated, perfectly transcribed: Allegri's *Misere*. Mozart had stolen it – in his head! Everyone was amazed, including the Pope – who was so amazed he quite forgot to excommunicate him.

The company of cardinals and the Pope and the imposing city of Rome did not have too much of an effect on Wolfgang. He was still a silly young boy, who was giggling his way around Italy. "I am well. God be thancked and praised" he wrote home, "and I kiss mamas hand and my sisters face, nose, neck, and my wretched pen, and her rear end if it's clean."

The Mozarts were a success all over the country. In Milan, Leopold got his dream: Wolfgang was commissioned — for money! — to write an opera. It was called *Mistridate* and set in Ancient Rome. On St Stephen's Day, 1770, it opened at the Opera House. Leopold was watching nervously from a box, Wolfgang himself — cool as a cucumber — was on the clavier. When the curtain came down, the applause went through the roof like a hurricane. The piece was such a hit it was performed every night for the next 20 nights. The feted composer was just fourteen years old.

This tour was different from the others. There were fewer performing tricks. He was being presented more as a composer than as a freakishly good performer.

It was while he was in Italy that Wolfgang's angelic voice broke — Leopold wrote home to his wife that the boy could no longer get "five clear notes". Mozart was still far from mature — "PS kiss mama's hands for me 1 000 000 000 000 times," he wrote. "Greetings to all good friends and a Thousand compliments to you from Diarrhea especially at the rear end". But he was moving towards adulthood. He was made a member of The Philharmonic Society of

Bologna. In Naples, he was presented with a medal, a bit like a knighthood. He grew taller and plumper and blossomed in the sunshine. He sailed on the Mediterranean and saw Vesuvius smoking. He wrote symphonies, airs and sonatas galore. Travel was broadening his mind.

Wolfgang fell so in love with the Italians that he changed his middle name in their honour. He had been christened Wolfgang Gottlieb – which was the German for "love of God". On this tour, he changed it to Wolfgang Amadeus – which means the same in Italian. He returned to Milan later in his life, although he was sadly never to travel through Italy again. But he would always be known as Wolfgang Amadeus Mozart.

CHAPTER SEVEN

The world in which Mozart lived was undergoing a period of great change. During his short lifetime, America got its independence and France had her revolution. The piano was invented in Italy and became instantly popular throughout Germany. Mozart now had a whole new instrument to work with. Back home in Salzburg, there were changes afoot at a local level which were to make his life a misery.

In March 1772, the old archbishop – the one who had supported the Mozarts on their tour of Italy – died. To everyone's surprise, Herr Hieronymous Colloredo was elected to take his place. Colloredo was a tall man, dark, imposing. He liked horses, and the ladies. He, too, was a man of the Enlightenment, and something of a musician. But he was also a stickler: he was determined to get the finances of Salzburg back on track, and keep the servants down. Servants were property, rather than people, to Colloredo. And musicians came under the heading of Servants, not Artists. He was known to be grumpy and, as soon as he was appointed, he became very grand. It was not long before he and Mozart were at loggerheads.

Wolfgang started off by being on his very best behaviour. He wrote a wonderful piece to celebrate Colloredo's enthronement. In his sixteenth year, he wrote seven symphonies as well as tons of church music. He was improving all the time – as a violinist

and pianist and composer. In August, the Archbishop made Mozart his official concert master. It was a job and it was recognition — the two things which Leopold had been craving for his son. But the money was poor — it was no more than he had been getting at fifteen as a violinist — and it was a tie to rotten old Salzburg.

The trouble with the Mozarts was that they had now seen the rest of Europe. They knew what was out there. They had dined with emperors and kings. They had swept through the corridors of Versailles. And they could see Salzburg for what it was — a small, provincial, unimportant place. They wanted more.

The trouble with Salzburg was that it had known this musical genius for too long. It had started to take him for granted. It had been proud of the child Mozart — he had been sweet and clever and famous. It was much less interested in the adult. So he kept composing all these nice tunes! It was not so very different from what he had been doing when he was twelve. And there were tons of composers all over the place, trotting out symphonies and sonatas, just like him. "Yet another example" said one pompous observer, "of early fruit being more extraordinary than excellent." In fact now they thought about it, this Mozart was turning into a bit of a disappointment.

And the trouble with Wolfgang was that, for him, composing was just too easy. For most people, writing music was a bit of an effort; for Wolfgang, it was nothing. One day, a younger music student asked him for advice on how to start composing.

"If one has the spirit of a composer", Mozart replied, rather grandly, "one writes because one cannot help it." The boy asked him if there were any books he might recommend on the subject, and Wolfgang started to lose patience. He pointed to his ears, his head and his heart: "That is your school! If all is right here, then you may take the pen without delay." He himself wrote music, he said, "as the pig grunts"; and someone else, he recalled, said "as the sparrow sings". It was a noise – a beautiful noise – that just came out of him. He simply had to do it; there was no choice. His head was constantly brimming with music. The only labour was to get it written down as quickly as he could.

Mozart stayed in Salzburg for three years. He was

desperate to impress the Archbishop, and wrote madly in this period – masses, litanies, serenades, clavier concertos, string quartets, violin concertos. But the more he wrote, the less impressed Archbishop Colloredo became. And if the new Archbishop was no fan of Mozart, then the rest of Salzburg wasn't going to pretend to be either. They had some sucking up to do and they took their lead from him. The general reaction to a new piece by Wolfgang Amadeus Mozart became: "So what?"

***

Leopold Mozart lay on his bed, head spinning, trying to keep the tears from his eyes. As the clatter of the horses' hooves grew fainter and the choking noise of Nannerl's sobs increased, he suddenly sat bolt upright. He hadn't even said goodbye!

He ran to the window, but it was too late. The coach, containing Wolfgang and Anna Maria, had already turned the corner of the cobbled street and passed through the city gate. Leopold collapsed back down again. They may never meet again, and he had not even kissed them farewell. It was the 27th of September, 1777: "such a melancholy day", he wrote "as I never thought all my life to experience."

But it had to be done. Wolfgang's situation in Salzburg had become ridiculous. When he was a boy, everyone had agreed that kings would be fighting to have the honour of employing him. Yet here he was, a young man, working for a minor Archbishop who couldn't care less. Wolfgang had to travel again, to try and find a proper, permanent job. Leopold was sure of that. He would stay behind and work for Colloredo until Wolfgang and Anna Maria were settled, then he and Nannerl would move to be with them.

This was the first time that the father had ever been parted from his beloved son. Leopold's pain was acute. And how on earth they would manage without him, he did not know. They were used to him sorting out everything. He was the one who understood big cities and powerful people. He had made all the decisions before now. He immediately sat down and wrote to them, trying to direct their every move. He told them where to stay, who to visit, what to wear –

adding that they should "get the servant always to put the boot-tree in the boots". They would miss his attention to detail, he shouldn't wonder. And he would miss them. He would miss his wife, and his son. But "what saddens me most", he said "is that I can't hear you play clavier or violin anymore."

If Leopold was down, though, Wolfgang was feeling up. He was delighted to see the back of Salzburg. To be home was to be in prison. Now, he was free. It was true that he was used to his father doing everything for him. And what a blessed relief it was to be away! He was 21 years old, after all. Time to make a few decisions for himself, thank you very much. Of course, he had mama along for the ride this time, but − let's face it − she was a pushover. As the carriage sped on its way, Mozart couldn't help but laugh with joy and excitement. At last, he was in charge. He had nothing but faith in his own future.

In fact, this tour was to be the most disastrous of his life. Their first stop was Munich, where they got a warm welcome, but no job. Leopold sent them on to Augsberg, where the welcome was even warmer. Wolfgang stopped in on the piano-maker, Herr Stein, and spent a happy afternoon playing, experimenting, on his exciting new keyboards. But there was still no job. So they headed on to Mannheim, where there was still no job. But that didn't bother Mozart. This was a city of music – it had the best orchestra in Europe – and it was teeming with musicians. He started making friends – real friends, as talented, almost, as him – and he began to live for the first time. He had no job, but he had a social life. And he discovered girls.

A music copyist called Herr Weber and his four delightful daughters were very welcoming to Wolfgang. They enjoyed many musical evenings. The eldest girl, Aloysia, had a particularly lovely voice. She was also a particularly lovely girl. While he played the piano, she sang along. And he fell in love. He might not find a paid position, he wrote to his papa, but he was sure he could make ends meet if he taught a lot, drank only water and just had fruit for pudding...

Wolfgang's letters were driving Leopold quite mad. He knew it! He knew they wouldn't be able to manage without him! He knew Wolfgang would go

off the rails. That boy was the only hope this family had, and he was talking of staying in Mannheim and eating fruit! He took out his pen and laid on the guilt: "You may see as clearly as the sun that the future condition of your aged parents and you sister depend on you," he wrote. "I devoted all my time to you two in the hope and indeed reliance of your care in return," he reminded. All he asked for was "a peaceful old age in which I might quietly await death". They must leave. Right now. "Away with you to Paris, and as speedily as you can..."

Chastened, Wolfgang did what he was told.

CHAPTER EIGHT

The Paris in which the Mozarts arrived in the spring of 1778 was very different to the one they remembered. For a start, it was one big puddle — very difficult to travel around in — and their lodgings were cold and horrid. It was also at war with itself — being torn apart both by politics and by musical differences. There was a big row raging at the time, about whether Italian or French music was the best. Composers were all conspiring against one another and none of them wanted Mozart to be a success.

Wolfgang did make friends, however, and again his social life started to get a bit wild. He was working hard. His marvellous *Paris Symphony* was written here and performed in June – the audience loved it so much that they actually burst into applause in the middle! But he was also partying hard, and neglecting his poor mama. The room they had taken was up a huge flight of stairs, and they couldn't get the clavier up it. So whenever Wolfgang was teaching, practising or composing – which was every waking hour – he had to be out. Anna Maria spoke no French and had very little money. So she stayed in all the time, horribly lonely.

One night, Wolfgang came home late to find his mother unwell. He was tired and caught up with his own affairs. He didn't think to call a doctor. When he came home the next night, he realised that she was really very ill. He did call a doctor, but too late. Anna Maria Mozart died, with her son at her side, in their lodgings in Paris on the 2nd of July, 1778. Leopold had been right to suffer so at their parting – he and his wife were, indeed, never to see each other again.

Wolfgang's behaviour that night was quite weird. He was overcome with guilt and terrified of how to break the news to his papa. So just decided not to do it all. At two o'clock in the morning, he wrote to

Leopold, warning him that Anna Maria wasn't feeling well. The doctor was with her, he hoped that she would pull through, they would just have to trust in God. With his mother's corpse laying beside him, he carried on happily with several pages of chatty news – "let's leave these mournful thoughts, let's turn to hope" – describing the performance of his symphony, and the ice cream he had eaten after it. The idea, in his grief and confusion, was that this letter would prepare the ground. He then wrote to a friend of Leopold's, telling him the truth – "Mourn with me! This was the saddest day of my life!" – and asking him to go round and break the news of poor Anna Maria's death.

It was the first time in his life that Wolfgang was alone, without either parent by his side. It was his first test of character as an adult. He failed it.

***

Mozart was miserable. He was 23 years old, he was back – he could hardly believe it himself – in wretched Salzburg, and he was in the dog house.

Since the disaster that was Paris, his papa seemed to have been in a permanent bad mood with him. Wolfgang liked to think positive but, these days, every time he came up with a brilliant new idea to solve all their problems, papa just shot him down in flames. "I am tired of your projects!" Leopold shouted at him. "From now on, I will make all the plans around here! You – you just spend all your time with fools and flatterers. You cannot tell tinsel from pure gold."

He was also heart-broken, though he couldn't own up to papa about that. On his way back to Salzburg, after his father had summoned him home in such a fury, he had stopped off in Augsberg to see the Webers. And there was Aloysia, quite caught up with another young man. She had no interest in Wolfgang at all.

He didn't think much of Papa's new "plan" either. In the light of Wolfgang's failure to find anything else, Leopold had gone, cap in hand, to Colloredo. He had secured a sort of package deal, where the Archbishop would employ both Mozarts. Leopold would continue in the orchestra, and Wolfgang would be concert-master, but he would be allowed time off to write opera when he needed it. The money was, as usual, not good. But if Nannerl continued as a piano teacher, then the three of them should be able to just about get by. After all his grand hopes, Leopold was once again reduced to making long calculations of how they might scrape together a pittance by working till they dropped.

For over a year, Wolfgang kept his head down. It wasn't in his nature to keep quiet – he was still giggly and over-excited and a constant fidget – but he did try not to get into trouble with either his father or his boss. He wrote a lot of fine church music, and two excellent symphonies and then – thank God! – an invitation arrived. In the summer of 1780, the Elector of Bavaria asked if he might come to Munich and write an opera.

Opera – the combination of music with a play – was quite a new, popular thing in Mozart's day. It was part of this Age of Enlightenment – taking music out of the church, and into the theatre. Ever since he had first started to experiment with it, as a young teenager, Wolfgang had adored opera. It suited him down to the ground. He loved working in the theatre, with actors and singers, costumes and scenery. He loved all the rehearsals and dramas. He was a highly emotional young man, and opera is an emotional form of music. Colloredo had to let him go – it was the only good part of Leopold's agreement. As soon as Wolfgang got the nod he was off.

Idomeneo – about an ancient King of Crete – was a rush job. Mozart got to Munich in November, started to write the music as the production went into rehearsal, and on the 26th of January was in the stalls for the first night. Leopold and Nannerl had joined him, too. As the orchestra struck the final, rousing chords and the audience leapt to its feet, they could feel proud of Wolfgang once more. Half of Salzburg seemed to be in the audience that night, and Leopold was mobbed by his fellow musicians. "That was the loveliest thing I have ever heard," wept one. Another said that the chorus was "so powerful no one could hear it in the greatest heat of summer without feeling as cold as ice." Leopold heard it all, and glowed.

After all that fuss and hard work, the opera was only put on for a few nights. In fact, Wolfgang only heard it once more in his life. But when it played, it played to a cheering, stomping crowd. Mozart's hopes were raised up once more. It was so nice to be back in a big city. And everybody loved him here. Surely, now, he must get work…

While he was in Munich he knocked off a few other pieces – a comic opera, and a mass. He was keen to show the Elector how versatile he was. But no job offer came. Instead, a new demand arrived from Archbishop Colloredo. The court of Salzburg was travelling to Vienna. Mozart must meet it there. Well, thought Wolfgang, at least it wasn't horrible Salzburg. But still, it was so annoying to get these commands. Here he was, Top Opera Writer, being bossed around like a slave.

And when he got to Vienna, he was even more annoyed. The Archbishop might have been pleased by the success of *Idomeneo*. After all, Mozart's success was his success. But he didn't see it like that. Colloredo was, in fact, deeply irritated. He just did not like his concert-master. That Mozart, he thought, was too big for his stumpy little boots. And when Mozart arrived, he would be put back firmly in his very low place.

So it was that Wolfgang found himself back in Vienna – the city where he had played in the palace gardens and sat on the lap of the Empress – being treated like a servant. He was given miserable, dark accommodation with the valets. He had to take all his meals in the servants' hall, though he was – he noted, wryly – seated just above the cooks. He was also refused permission to perform for anyone but the Archbishop. When the Emperor invited him to play, he had to refuse. When he could have played a concert for money, he was not allowed.

In May 1781, as the Archbishop was preparing to return to Salzburg, he called Mozart to his chamber. He had heard that his concert master was planning to stay on, alone, in Vienna. He had finally had enough. While he looked cool, inside his blood was boiling.

"Well, young fellow, when are you off?" he asked, cordially.

"I had wanted to leave tonight, your Highness, but all the seats were taken," replied Mozart, sounding respectful but lying through his teeth. And they were the last civil words that passed between them.

The Archbishop went mad: "You are the most worthless fellow I know! Out! Now! You scoundrel! You lousy rogue! I want nothing more to do with such miserable scum. There is the door!"

"And I want nothing more to do with you!" bellowed Mozart in return. "I just hope this decision is final!"

And with that, Wolfgang Mozart was thrown, with a kick up the bum, onto the streets of Vienna — a court musician no more.

Chapter Nine

Leopold sat at home in Salzburg, wringing his hands with worry. Wolfgang may have been 25 years old, but he was still no more grown-up than he had been when he had come home from Paris. He may have been a musical genius, but he did not have an ounce of common sense. However much Leopold had tried, he was unable to drill any sense of responsibility into that boy's skull. How on earth was he going to cope with all the practical difficulties of life as a freelance musician? He wrote long letters to Vienna, outlining all the problems that Wolfgang was going to face: he had to earn every penny and then collect it. He had to run his own household and manage all his money. He had to stop getting on the wrong side of people who were in a position to save his life.

"Yes, yes, yes," replied his son. Wolfgang was so high with the relief of being free at last, that he could not look down at any of the problems on the road ahead. Papa knew he was a great composer. He would teach the piano and the violin, and write the sort of popular music that everyone wanted these days. He would be fine. "And, if you don't mind," he added "unless I have something particularly important to tell you, I shall only write to you once a week from now on. I am very busy just now." He had got away from the Archbishop, he was now slipping the clutches of his father. Mozart was moving into a whole new phase.

He was not, however, planning on spending it entirely alone. When Colloredo kicked him out, Mozart moved in with his old friends, the Webers. The lovely Aloysia was married now, and enjoying great success as a singer. But her younger sister Constanze was very much at home. She was nowhere near as pretty as her sister. In fact, she was extremely plain. But she had lovely eyes and a cheerful nature. And anyway, what price would Mozart fetch on the marriage market?

Apart from having no job and no money, Mozart was a pretty odd-looking creature. He had had such beauty as a child, but not as an adult. He was still small, thin and very pale. He had a fine head of hair, but, according to the fashion of the time, that was covered with a white wig. He had nice long eyelashes, but they fluttered astride an over-sized nose, on his very large head. He was also very silly. He swore like a trooper. He made daft jokes and giggled too much. He twitched a lot, and wriggled. But, despite all that, Constanze Weber thought he was wonderful. He just had to get his career going in Vienna, and then they could be married.

Joseph II was now the Emperor of Austria. Wolfgang admired him tremendously and longed to work for him full-time. The Emperor liked Mozart, too, but there were a number of reasons why he would not hire him. The first was the strong advice of his mother. Maria Theresa had never forgotten the disgusting way that Leopold had forced little

Wolfgang to play for her, when he was clearly terribly sick. From that moment, she had taken against the Mozart family – grasping sort of people, she felt. Not what they wanted at their court.

And then there was the problem of the musicians that the Emperor had already gathered around him. The conflict over music that he had seen in France was now raging all over Europe: did you like the Italians? Or did you like the rest? The Italians had already got themselves well in with this Emperor, and they were not letting him out of their clutches. Salieri, Righini, Anfossi, Martini – these composers are only known now as the enemies of Mozart, the people who kept him down. But back then, in Vienna in the 1780s, they were all the bee's knees. They could see that this Mozart was a threat, and they took every opportunity to poison the Emperor's mind against him.

Nevertheless, Joseph II fancied himself as a man of culture. He would not give Mozart a job, but he would give him a commission. He summoned Mozart to court and demanded an opera, please, in German this time, for his brand new theatre. Mozart set to work in a flurry and in July 1782, *The Abduction of the Seraglio* was at last performed. As the curtain came down and the applause roared around him, Mozart ran round to the door of the royal box to receive the Emperor's congratulations. He was to be disappointed. Joseph had indeed found the music beautiful, but "too beautiful for our ears", he moaned.

"Too beautiful?" challenged Mozart, trying to hide his disappointment. "Yes", complained the Emperor. "Too many notes, dear Mozart. Too many notes…" And he swept past, with the composer muttering, "Just as many as are necessary, your Majesty", to the retreating, imperial back.

Despite the Emperor's lack of appreciation, the opera was a great success. Wolfgang now had a name, and 1200 florins. He was in great demand to write pieces for people to promenade and dance to on a Viennese evening. The piano was all the rage these days, and Mozart was writing popular pieces for it. And he had a list of pupils as long as his arm. It was still a terrific struggle to make ends meet, but he was on the brink of success. Even Leopold couldn't complain too much. So at last, on the 4th of August, 1782 Wolfgang Amadeus Mozart and Constanze Weber were finally to marry.

***

The four-room second-floor apartment that was the Mozart marital home was in a state of complete chaos. It always was. Wolfgang didn't give a fig for tidiness, and his wife cared even less. Writing music now was no different from when he had written his first concerto back in papa's study: the ink flew everywhere, sheets of paper were flung all over the floor to dry. The couple loved to entertain and their riotous evenings generally ended up back here, with friends drinking and carousing late into the night. Connie tended to feel too delicate to clear up first thing. Piano pupils were always coming and going, treading the wretched Viennese dust into the floor. There was non-stop music – Wolfgang played and wrote with every waking minute. And there were always people; he hated being alone, and could write a masterpiece quite happily while he played billiards with his friends. Wolfgang could have done with marrying a female version of his father: someone sensible, who was good with money and could think ahead. In fact, in Constanze, he had managed to find someone even more hopeless than himself.

This morning, though, of the 12th of February, 1785 Constanze Mozart was going through the apartment like a dose of salts. Wolfgang was still sleeping off the riot that was the night before, and his wife was in a flap. Leopold Mozart was due to arrive any minute. He was coming to stay for six weeks. She had only met her father-in-law once before, on a visit to Salzburg, and it had not been a success. She knew he didn't approve of her, but this time she was going to show him. She would not give him one single opportunity to look down his long Austrian nose.

Indeed, from the moment he arrived, Leopold was pleasantly surprised. Constanze would not have been his choice of bride for his son, but they were happy together, anyone could see that. Their baby, little Karl, was a delight. And his Wolfgang was really rather successful out here. Leopold was here to attend a series of his subscription concerts, where people paid quite a lot to get in, and heard a new piece every time. He was horrified to find, the night before the premiere of the *Concerto in D minor*, that Wolfgang had not quite finished writing it yet. It quite ruined his enjoyment of the performance. "Relax, papa", said his son. "It makes it more exciting. It really is a premiere if even the composer has never heard it before!"

And twice, Leopold got a genuine thrill, when he could burst again with pride in his son, as he had done years before. Once he was at the finale of another concerto and saw Emperor Joseph II leap to his feet in applause and shout "Bravo!"

"The tears came into my eyes," he wrote back to Nannerl.

The other was when he met the most important living composer of the time, Joseph Haydn. Haydn had become a great friend to Wolfgang in Vienna. Indeed, Wolfgang called him "Papa Haydn" – he was the only musical guide, beside Leopold, that Mozart ever had. Haydn took Leopold's hand and looked into his eyes. "I must tell you", he said, "before God, and as an honest man, that I think your son the greatest composer I ever heard."

Leopold still wished that his son was better off — as a poor man himself, he valued financial comfort. But he could see that Wolfgang had carved out a decent life for himself in Vienna. When the two men shook hands and embraced at the end of that March, most of their differences were behind them. They were never to meet again. Leopold Mozart died a few years later. He was spared the knowledge that his two brilliant children, of whom he expected so much, were to quarrel badly over his will.

Chapter Ten

On the 1st of May 1786, Wolfgang Amadeus Mozart took up his baton and led the orchestra in the opening, quiet chords of his brand new opera *The Marriage of Figaro*. Mozart was dressed for the occasion – in a crimson silk suit and a hat trimmed with gold lace – and trembling with nerves. This opera was his biggest test so far. Most of musical Vienna was in the audience – Haydn was there, and Gluck. The Emperor sat, resplendent, in his royal box. And all of Mozart's enemies were there, too – Salieri, Martini, all the gang – longing for him to fail.

It had been a struggle getting this far. The Italians at court had advised the Emperor that he should never commission an opera from that upstart Mozart. And the story of *The Marriage of Figaro* was not at all popular in Vienna. It had been written by a Frenchman, for a start, and it suggested that powerful people like Emperors were a bad thing, and poor people were good. But Abbe da Ponte, an important Italian writer, persuaded Joseph that it should be done. He wrote the words and Mozart wrote the music – all in the space of six weeks.

The Emperor was looking forward to this premiere. He had enjoyed the arguments over whether it should be done; he always liked setting the cat among the pigeons in his court. Also, Mozart had visited him at the palace the other week and played a few of the pieces on the piano. They had sounded quite delightful.

So Mozart and Joseph were both quite startled when the opera began, and it sounded absolutely dreadful. The orchestra was out of tune, the singers were weak and kept forgetting their words. Mozart kept trying to control them – they had sounded wonderful in rehearsals. By the end of Act One, the audience was hissing and Mozart realised what had happened. He slipped from the orchestra and ran up to the royal box. "Your Majesty!" he spluttered. "Forgive me! The singers and the orchestra are all conspiring. They are ruining the opera on purpose! Please, your Majesty, do something!"

The Emperor did. One of Mozart's enemies had bribed all the musicians to give a bad performance, and the audience to hiss. One word from Joseph II and they were back on their best behaviour. The rest of the premiere went according to plan and the

encores lasted till dawn. *The Marriage of Figaro* is still considered to be the perfect opera of the Enlightenment – all light, glitter and wit. The songs from it were instant hits, they were sung in bars and danced to in village squares all over Europe. But it didn't make Mozart rich. He was getting more and more popular, but he still was not rich.

Money was coming into the Mozart's apartment – but it was flowing straight out again. Wolfgang felt that, with his life at court and around the aristocracy, he needed to look and live the part. Constanze agreed, and had absolutely no sense about money anyway. They bought each other presents they could not afford and lived in a social whirl. Since Leopold's departure, life in their Viennese home had gone back to its previous chaos. Constanze was often ill, and took to her bed. Once, she didn't get up for eight months. She had had six difficult pregnancies and bad births; four of their babies had died. They now had two little boys.

But somehow, through all that noise and commotion, Mozart managed to work brilliantly. His work seemed to feed on chaos. He wrote in the mornings in his wife's sick room, with doctors and nurses around. He wrote in the evenings, while playing billiards with his friends. He left the afternoons free for his pupils, and the occasional pilgrim – though they never got much attention. One winter's afternoon in 1786, a young man arrived who Mozart had promised to listen to. In a typical muddle, Mozart had totally forgotten he was coming. He sat the student at the piano and rushed around the apartment collecting his things, as he was about to rush out. But, as soon as he heard the piano from the other room, he stopped dead in his tracks. For once, he – Wolfgang Amadeus Mozart – was impressed. "You mark my words," he said to his wife later. "We'll be hearing more from this Ludwig von Beethoven."

Mozart had promised to put on his next opera in Prague. In September 1787, he announced that it was ready, and he and his wife set off. In fact, he had not written a single note of it. It was ready – it was called *Don Giovanni* – but the whole thing existed only in his own head! They arrived in Prague to pleasant autumn weather, and Mozart wrote happily away in the garden of a friend, whilst playing a game of bowls. Every time it was his go, he had to get up from the manuscript and lob a ball. He finished most of the music with a week to spare for rehearsals. Nevertheless it wasn't quite complete. The night before the premiere, the producer found him drinking away merrily at a party.

"Where is the overture?" he bellowed into Mozart's ear. "I need my overture. Have you got it?"

"Yes" Mozart bellowed back. "It's all ready, in here," and he pointed at his head.

Constanze marched him back to their rooms and kept him awake all night as he wrote it down. The first time the orchestra saw the music was when the copyists ran into the theatre with it as the performance began. It was, as ever, a triumph.

***

One hot, thundery summer's afternoon, Mozart was working alone at home when there came a loud knock at the door. He opened it to find a tall figure, dressed head to toe in black, his face in shadow. The stranger thrust an envelope into Mozart's hand, and vanished back into the street. In the envelope was a letter, commissioning Mozart to write a requiem — music to be played at a funeral. It promised a decent sum, but commanded that the musician must never, ever ask for whom he was writing it. The year was 1791 — the best professional year of Mozart's life, and the year of his death.

Mozart was very busy that summer. He had two operas on the go: *The Magic Flute*, a light, jolly piece; and *The Clemency of Tito*, a more serious one written for the coronation of the new Emperor, Leopold II. He had had a busy year. For the carnival in January, he had produced 35 minuets, as well as countless waltzes. He had just finished a quintet for violins and returned to the stage as a pianist with a brand new concerto.

The past two years had been pretty grim for Wolfgang. Money had been tight, the Emperor Joseph had not been friendly and Constanze had found herself having to sell her jewellery to pay for Mozart to go on tour. He had got very depressed, and rather wayward again: drinking too much and staying out too late. But he was determined that 1791 would be different. Enough of wallowing in his sorrows. There was a new emperor on the throne, a new mood in Europe and it was time to turn over a new leaf. From now on it would be "Work! Work! Work!" he promised Constanze. "And what a delicious life we will lead."

He had no choice but to accept this commission of a requiem – they needed every florin they could get. He was also rather intrigued by it. As soon as he read the letter, the music started to form in his head. This could be marvellous, he thought to himself. This could be one of the greatest things I have ever written...

But first he had to get on with these operas. The Emperor had only just asked him for *The Clemency of Tito*, and he had 18 days to get to Prague and write the thing. He always loved going to Prague – they liked him there – but this was not one of his better trips. The opera was a grand and serious work; Wolfgang was very proud of it. But the audience was not impressed. They were there for the coronation, in the mood for a party – not a sermon. So that was quite stressful. And he wasn't really feeling very well.

When he got back to Vienna, he only had a couple of weeks to get *The Magic Flute* ready. The premiere for this, on the 30th of September, was a huge success. Mozart was conducting, the orchestra was full of his friends, his sister-in-law was singing on stage and the audience loved him. It was one of the happiest nights of his life. He had just a few niggling worries. The first was that the stranger had popped up again, demanding his funeral music. And the other was that he still wasn't feeling very well.

***

That winter, Mozart devoted to this requiem. Actually, he couldn't stop himself. The music was billowing up in his mind, demanding to be written out on the page. It had a life of its own. But it was an awful struggle. He was feeling really terrible. *The Magic Flute* was still playing to packed houses, but Mozart was not the conductor. He was too weak to leave the house now. He spent all evening in his bed – hearing the opera in his mind, tapping the rhythm on the sheets – feverish and frustrated.

By November, he could only dictate the music, he was too feeble to hold his pen. Constanze and her sister stood by his bedside, singing parts of it as he directed them. He sank back on his pillow. "I am sure" he gasped "that I am composing this requiem for myself."

The requiem was never finished. Wolfgang Amadeus Mozart died in his wife's arms, shortly after midnight on the 5th of December, 1791. In just 35 years, he had written over 60 symphonies, 30-odd

piano concertos, wonderful church music, hundreds of dances and seven brilliant operas. He had indeed brought music into the Age of Enlightenment. Yet, he was buried, with little ceremony, in an unmarked, common grave. He left his family nothing but the immortality of the Mozart name.

TIMELINE

1756: Wolfgang Mozart is born in Salzburg, Austria on the 27th January

1762: The Mozart family arrive in Vienna to show their children's talents to Viennese society, including the Empress of Austria

1763: The Mozarts embark on their next European tour

1767, Easter: Mozart aged 11 writes a mass for the Archbishop of Salzburg

1769, December: Leopold and Wolfgang set off on a new tour of Italy

1770: Wolfgang's opera *Mistridate* is performed at the opera house in Milan. He is 14 years old

1777: Wolfgang and Anna Maria leave Salzburg again to find a permanent job for Wolfgang

1778, 2nd July: Anna Maria Mozart dies in Paris

1780, Summer: the Elector of Bavaria invites Wolfgang to Munich to write an opera

1782, 4th August: Wolfgang, aged 25, marries Constanze Weber in Vienna

1786, 1st May: Wolfgang conducts his brand new opera, *Marriage of Figaro,* in Vienna

1791, 5th December: Wolfgang dies, aged 35

Who Was Wolfgang Amadeus Mozart?

After you've finished the book, test yourself and see how well you remember what you've read.

1. Why was the 18th century called the Age of Enlightenment?
   Because the light bulb was invented during this period
   Because it became fashionable to go on a diet
   Because people started to question their understanding of the world

2. A favourite toy of the infant Wolfgang was:
   A piece of chalk and a slate
   A signed photo of his favourite pianist
   A wooden spoon and a saucepan to drum on

3. At first, Mozart's parents thought he might grow up to be:
   An orchestral musician
   A landscape gardener
   A professional mathematician

4. Wolfgang and his sister Nannerl's pet canary could:
   Whistle *Air on a G string*
   Sing on a G sharp
   Rap along to G-Unit

5. How long did it take the four-year-old Wolfgang to learn to play a complicated piece of music by Wagenseil?
    30 minutes
    3 hours
    3 days

6. What game did Wolfgang and Nannerl most enjoy playing while they were travelling?
    I-Spy
    Mario
    Create-a-kingdom

7. When the young Wolfgang first met the Empress Maria Theresa, he:
    Fell to his knees and took off his hat
    Jumped on her lap and gave her a kiss
    Refused to shake her hand because he was in a sulk

8. What happened to the princess who Wolfgang offered to marry?
    She was executed during the French revolution
    She was sent away to a Swiss convent
    She ran off to join a travelling circus

9 . When he played to the Queen of France, Wolfgang wore:
    A sequinned waistcoat and high-heeled boots
    A leather jacket and shades
    A silk suit and a ceremonial sword

10. What was the occasion for Mozart's first symphony?
    To celebrate the Olympics game in Salzburg
    To commemorate the birth of Queen Charlotte's 15th child
    As a get-well present for his father

11. Leopold Mozart thought London was a dangerous place because:
    Young men in hooded garments roamed the streets
    The people had no religion and were badly brought up
    The food was often unsafe to eat because of the lack of refrigeration

12. The first opera written by Mozart was called:
    The Pretend Idiot
    The Ersatz Prince
    The False Witness

13. What did Mozart do after hearing the *Misere* sung in the Sistine Chapel?
    Begged his father to allow him to join the Pope's choir
    Wrote the complicated music down on paper for the first time
    Turned the melody into a theme song for Roma FC

14. What piece of advice did Leopold give his son and wife when they went off on tour on their own

Always eat with your mouth closed
Make sure the servant looks after the boots properly
Hide a copy of your passports in a safe place

15. How did Wolfgang suggest cutting expenses to enable him to marry Aloysia, the girl he fancied?
    By travelling by donkey instead of in a carriage
    By sacking their servant and getting his mother to clean the boots
    By eating only fruit for pudding

16. When his mother died in Paris in 1778, Wolfgang:
    Wrote an opera based on her life story
    Pretended that she was still alive
    Asked the city authorities to name a Metro station after her

17. When Mozart went to Vienna with Archbishop Colloredo, he was:
    Treated as an honoured guest and given his own suite in the palace
    Made to eat his meals in the servants' hall
    Mobbed by fans eager to get his autograph

18. Mozart thought that Constanze Weber:
    Was a great beauty with a fantastic figure
    Had a cheerful nature and lovely eyes
    Would be able to manage his career for him

19. The first performance of *The Marriage of Figaro* was nearly ruined because:

   The singers and orchestra were bribed to perform badly
   The sprinkler system went off and soaked the audience
   Mozart forgot his glasses and couldn't see to conduct the music

20. In 1791 Mozart was commissioned to write a requiem by:

   The winner of the annual Viennese lottery
   A mysterious stranger dressed in black
   The famous Austrian actor, Arnold Schwarzenegger

Dear Reader,

No matter how old you are, good books always leave you wanting to know more. If you have any questions you would like to ask the author, **Gill Hornby**, about **Mozart** please write to us at: SHORT BOOKS 15 Highbury Terrace, London N5 1UP.

If you enjoyed this title, then you would probably enjoy others in the series. Why not click on our website for more information and see what the teachers are being told? **www.shortbooks.co.uk**

All the books in the WHO WAS… series are available from TBS, Distribution Centre, Colchester Road, Frating Green, Colchester, Essex CO7 7DW
(Tel: 01206 255800), at £4.99 + P&P.

Other titles in the WHO WAS... series:

WILLIAM SHAKESPEARE
The Mystery of the World's Greatest Playwright
Rupert Christiansen

Everyone has heard of plays like *Macbeth* and *A Midsummer Night's Dream*. But why do we know so little about the man who wrote them? Who exactly was William Shakespeare from Stratford-upon-Avon, and why do so many people believe that he was not the person he seemed to be?

This book is an exciting detective story, which goes back over four hundred years to the dramatic events of the reign of Queen Elizabeth I and explores the way that a brilliant and ambitious young man was caught up in a violent world of murder, revenge and treason.

ISBN: 1-904095-34-8

QUEEN VICTORIA
The Woman who Ruled the World
Kate Hubbard

Victoria was just 18 when she was crowned Queen in 1837 – a tiny figure with a will of iron. Never was there so queenly a queen. She made Britain great, and the people loved her for it.

In 1861 tragedy struck, when her husband Albert died. The little Queen loved dogs and cream cakes and the troops who fought her wars, but most of all she loved Albert. Dumb with grief, she hid herself away. Suddenly it seemed the woman who had made the monarchy so strong would destroy it. Could anyone persuade Victoria to be Queen again?

ISBN: 1-904095-32-1

Gill Hornby lives with her husband and four children in Kintbury, Berkshire. She is also the author of *WHOWAS... Jane Austen: The Girl with the Magic Pen* (Short Books, 2005)